The Spirit and the Bride Say,

"COME!"

DESTINY IMAGE BOOKS BY JOHN AND CAROL ARNOTT

The Spirit and Bride Say, "Come!"
Preparing for the Glory
Essential Training for Preparing for the Glory
Soaking in the Spirit
Soaking Encounter Journal
Grace and Forgiveness

The Spirit and the Bride Say,

"COME!"

Prophetic Dreams that Prepare You for Jesus' Second Coming and the Greater Glory Outpouring

CAROL ARNOTT

DESTINY IMAGE® PUBLISHERS, INC.

P.O. Box 310, Shippensburg, PA 17257-0310

"Promoting Inspired Lives."

This book and all other Destiny Image and Destiny Image Fiction books are available at Christian bookstores and distributors worldwide.

For more information on foreign distributors, call 717-532-3040.

Reach us on the Internet: www.destinyimage.com.

ISBN 13 TP: 978-0-7684-6104-6
ISBN 13 eBook: 978-0-7684-6105-3
ISBN 13 HC: 978-0-7684-6107-7
ISBN 13 LP: 978-0-7684-6106-0

For Worldwide Distribution, Printed in the U.S.A.

2 3 4 5 6 7 8 / 26 25 24 23 22

The Spirit and the Bride say, "Come." And let the one who hears say, "Come." And let the one who is thirsty come; let the one who desires take the water of life without price (Revelation 22:17).

CONTENTS

FOREWORD

I am deeply impacted and moved by Carol Arnott's book, *The Spirit and the Bride Say, "Come!"* Carol has been a dear personal friend and close partner in soaking prayer for almost twenty-five years. I have seen the Holy Spirit move in a glorious way through her life and ministry, impacting millions of people around the world. Because of the great outpouring of the Spirit in Toronto, we felt empowered to feed the hungry, comfort the afflicted, and reach people with the message and love of Jesus in some of the darkest situations on earth. Both Rolland and I were greatly transformed through the movement that Carol and John Arnott led. Carol's book draws us to a deeper intimacy with God, inviting us to lay our lives down in total surrender to our Lord and Bridegroom King. As we seek to go deeper in the river of God's presence, He enables us to endure all the trials that hit us along the way. As I've said from the pulpit many times before, there was a time when I could easily imagine myself burned out, leaving Mozambique, and going back home to work at a Kmart! But I thank God over and over again for refreshing us through the beautiful move of the Spirit that the Arnotts were given to steward.

Carol is one of the most intimate lovers of God I've ever met. What she shares in her book is a convicting message of holiness, and it certainly should be. But what I love most about her call to a life of purity is the reason for it, and the way we have to seek it: in ever deeper intimacy with God. More important than any outward discipline or method is the goal of our faith: Jesus Himself— knowing Him, reflecting Him, offering ourselves in joy, full of pure oil, to be His hands and feet in the world.

Where I live we face many pressures. So many people are in severe need that it could easily overwhelm me on any given day. I'm just one little person, and yet I'm aware that real fruitfulness always comes from intimacy with God. As you lay your life down for the Lord and offer Him whatever's in your hands, He will accept it and multiply it. This is something Carol and I share at the deepest level. Because of this, to this day we soak and pray together over the phone nearly every week. We have enjoyed countless hours quietly seeking God's presence because we believe that simply being able to attend to the Father and soak in His Spirit is an incredibly precious gift. In fact, we feel compelled to spend this time. It is made possible by grace, and draws us by grace. In these times of intimate prayer that go beyond words, God moves us closer to His Son. We know that without daily grace from heaven, nothing we can do ever works out the way we would like or bears the kind of fruit we hope for. We want to live a pure life, but His presence is what purifies. We talk about being "undone" in prayer because in these times He will remove the things that stand between us and Him. In this way He loves to create a new heart in His children, soft and alive.

This is not simply some new and special discovery of the charismatic church, or of a recent revival, or something that belongs to this or that denomination. I believe that the what Carol calls soaking—the quiet prayer of the heart—has belonged to the church from the beginning. It is for every believer who wants it. It was cherished by ancient Christian monks in the desert, by priests and laymen, in monasteries and mission fields and private homes by believers throughout the centuries. It has been practiced by Orthodox and Catholics and Protestants and saints in every part of the world. Psalm 46:10 tells us, *"Be still and know that I am God."* Jesus Himself spent long periods of time praying secretly in the wilderness. When you know why He did this, you will not want to live without it. Soaking prayer, the prayer of the heart, brings food from heaven. Justice is there, and purity, and comfort from the Father, and everything else we need.

Jesus said, *"Which of you, if your son asks for bread, will give him a stone? Or if he asks for a fish, will give him a snake? If you, then, though you are evil, know how to give good gifts to your children, how much more will your Father in heaven give good gifts to those who ask him!"* (Matthew 7:9-11). Sometimes we may ask for things that are bad for us, or that we are not ready for, and in His mercy, we do not get them. When you ask God for what is good, He is always pleased, and His presence is the greatest thing we could ever ask for. It's always right to ask for this. It's always a good time to seek it. It's His presence that teaches us what else is good and healthy to ask for, or where we should go, or what we should do or take or leave behind.

The Spirit and the Bride indeed say "Come." I pray that Carol's humble and powerful words will inspire you, as they have so often inspired me, to lay down your life. Not just for duty, but for intimacy with the only one who is worthy.

HEIDI G. BAKER, PH.D.
Co-founder and Executive Chairman
of the Board, Iris Global

INTRODUCTION

Jesus references His return for His Bride many times in Scripture. Here are three verses:

> *"Let us be glad and rejoice and give Him glory, for the marriage of the Lamb has come, and His wife has made herself ready."* *And to her it was granted to be arrayed in fine linen, clean and bright, for the fine linen is the righteous acts of the saints* (Revelation 19:7-8 NKJV).

Then he said to me, "Write: 'Blessed are those who are called to the marriage supper of the Lamb!'" And he said to me, "These are the true sayings of God" (Revelation 19:9 NKJV).

But while they were on their way to buy the oil, the groom came, and those who were ready went in with him to the wedding feast; and the door was shut (Matthew 25:10 NASB).

When the Toronto Blessing revival began in 1994, the Lord gave me a vision that included the Wedding Feast of the Lamb. That vision continues to have a powerful impact on my husband John and me to this day.

Then in 2010, He gave me a life-changing dream concerning the next wave of Glory He wants to pour out on earth before He gathers His Bride, who has made herself ready.

These dreams, along with Scripture and insights from the Lord concerning end-time events, have given us greater revelation of Jesus' desire for union with His Bride—one who is *passionately* in love with Him. We have also seen how eager our heavenly Father is to present His Son with a Bride who has "eyes only for Him" (see Ps. 141:8 TPT) and is without spot or wrinkle (see Eph. 5:27), untainted by the enemy and the greed of this world.

> OUR HEAVENLY FATHER
> IS EAGER TO PRESENT HIS
> SON WITH A BRIDE WHO IS
> WITHOUT SPOT OR WRINKLE.

I pray that this book will stir your heart to make yourself ready for His outpouring of Glory, for the mighty end-time harvest, and to be the Bride of Jesus without spot or wrinkle.

Chapter 1

THE TEST

It was Mother's Day, the night before my birthday, in May 2010. John, my husband, was away traveling, and I wasn't feeling all that great, but I was looking forward to my son Michael coming from Stratford to Toronto to celebrate with me. Then during the day he phoned to say he had been called in to work and couldn't get out of it. With this news, and now also feeling a little down and discouraged, I went to bed and said to the Lord, "I'm not going to set my alarm. If You want me to go to church, You wake me up." (Really not a good idea to give the Lord an ultimatum.)

It was an unusual night. I had a dream, extraordinary in intensity and especially vivid in detail. It was sobering, and the fear of the Lord was piercing.

At times in the dream, I didn't know if people were going to make it out alive from the intensity of what was happening. Upon waking from this vivid dream, I rolled over and looked at the clock. It said 9:45 a.m. I thought, *I've missed church*, because church would start at 10:30, and it would take me an hour to get ready and get there. I was still very conscious of the realistic dream and thought, *I need to get my tablet, or a piece of paper, or something to write this down, so I don't forget any details.* I could still feel the weight and the urgency of the dream.

> I COULD STILL FEEL
> THE WEIGHT AND THE
> URGENCY OF THE DREAM.

OBEDIENCE

Our bed is quite high, so I have to slide my way out of it, but as my feet were about to touch the floor, I heard the audible voice of God say, "Carol, get up! Have a shower! Do your hair! Get your clothes on! Have a quick breakfast, and get down to the church. Now!"

In that moment all my possible excuses evaporated. I had heard the audible voice of the Lord once before when I was saved. That time it was the loving voice of Jesus repeating the 23rd Psalm. But this was the voice of the Father—the voice of authority. It was very strong and very directive, firm yet full of love. When He said, "Get out of bed," I got moving! I could think of nothing but the urgent voice of my heavenly Father. If you think the roadrunner is fast, I think I left him in the dust as I never got ready so quickly in my life.

I jumped in the car, but I still hadn't recorded the dream. I knew that somewhere on my phone was a recording device. I'm not technically inclined, so figuring out the recorder on the fly was a bit of a challenge. I got to the recording app, found the record button, and started dictating what I had dreamt. I drove, dodging traffic and praying, "God, please, please Lord, let the traffic lights be green! And please Lord, put an angel with me because I'm going a little fast. Don't let the police see me." (Again, not recommended.) I did all the things one shouldn't do, but God was kind. I only got one red light of the ten or more along that route.

I was a bit late getting there, and the parking lot was full. *Agh! Where am I going to park?* I fretted. *Is anyone in my spot?* Thankfully, my parking space was clear. I parked, jumped out of my car, and raced into the church. A baby dedication had just ended and worship was starting. *I'll sit at the back,* I thought, but the Lord said, *No!*

"Okay Lord," I whispered. There usually was a seat beside the worship team. *I'll go and sit there,* I decided. But as I started up the aisle the Lord said, *I want you to sit in your seat at the front.*

There will be someone sitting in my seat, I objected.

Well then, tell them to move!

"Oh! Okay God," I said, my heart pounding.

I cut across and up to the front row. And as I rounded the corner I saw two people sitting in the seats where John and I usually sit. To this day I don't know who they were, but when they saw me, they instantly jumped up and moved. I'm not sure what the expression on my face was, but they moved quickly! With great relief I sat down in my seat. "Whew, I'm here, now what?"

And then the thought hit me. "Lord, are we doing the dream today?" I asked.

The idea of sharing the dream with the people made me uneasy. I shivered. It was such an intense message, I felt like both I and the congregation had to be ready for it.

THE IDEA OF SHARING
THE DREAM WITH THE
PEOPLE MADE ME UNEASY.

I had been so focused on getting to the church that I didn't imagine God might ask me to share the dream that morning. Now the question came to me—was the dream a foreshadowing of what would happen in our church when I shared it with the people? I trembled at the thought, knowing just how overwhelming it had been and what could happen.

I then heard Him say, *No. This is a test of your obedience.*

Simultaneously, I sighed with relief and was oh, so thankful I had been obedient to get to the church quickly. Pastor Sandra Long, noticing that something was going on between the Lord and me said, "You have something to share prophetically? Why don't you come up and share it?"

As I walked to the platform, the Lord said, *I don't want you to share it now. You can share it generally, just a little bit.* So I did just that.

That day, my heavenly Father took me by the hand and led me through what He wanted me to do and say. He didn't speak with a still small voice. His words were clear and directive and oh, so loving. I knew I could trust Him.

A year and half later, as I was preparing for a conference, the Lord said, *I want you to share the dream.* It would be the first time I shared the full dream publicly.

> THAT DAY, MY HEAVENLY FATHER TOOK ME BY THE HAND AND LED ME THROUGH WHAT HE WANTED ME TO DO AND SAY.

Chapter 2

THE DREAM: WHITE HOT HOLINESS

In the dream I was worshiping at the front of our church in what felt like a conference. The building was packed. I remember standing closer to the stage than I usually would, just in front of the podium. Worship was wonderful. I was drawn into God's presence, completely focused on Jesus and His love for me.

All of a sudden I felt like I was physically turning and being lifted off the ground. I opened my eyes and saw a whirlwind swirling rapidly around me, like standing still in eye of a hurricane, while everything around me was spinning. I was being lifted up and up and up and up, close to the ceiling.

Oh God, I thought, *am I going through the roof? Ahhh Lord, where are You taking me?*

Just as I reached the ceiling, I came down slowly, landing softly on my feet in front of the podium. At that moment, it felt like something was forcefully taken off of me and something else was firmly placed on me. My immediate thought was, *I think timidity and hesitancy just left me. I feel boldness and strength!*

> FROM THAT MOMENT THE
> WEIGHT OF HOLINESS
> AND THE FEAR OF THE
> LORD SETTLED ON ME.

From that moment the weight of holiness and the fear of the Lord settled on me. I grabbed the microphone off the front of the stage and, with great courage and authority, unlike my natural personality, declared to the people:

"Many of you here are doing things that grieve and displease the Lord. You've said, 'It's okay, God will forgive me because He's so loving. I can make it right with Him later. It's probably not a big deal.' But you have been using the grace of the Lord for your own agenda and purposes. It is unsanctified grace and mercy.

"The Lord says He is calling us to a new walk—to a new holiness. It is not a holiness of outward striving and performance. Rather, it's an inward conviction and holiness of the heart based on the Father's love."

As I scanned the room full of people, I said, "There is another Glory Cloud of His presence coming. In this cloud there will be the awesome, reverent fear of the Lord. For the fear of the Lord is the beginning of wisdom."

> THE LORD IS CALLING
> US TO A NEW WALK—
> TO A NEW HOLINESS.

As I uttered those words, I glanced up and saw a Glory cloud forming, and it was beginning to descend. It looked like an electric, fiery mist.

The power in the cloud was penetrating, severe, and unstoppable. My spirit gasped within me. I had not expected the cloud to appear that quickly. People weren't prepared!

A feeling of panic and urgency seized me. "Oh, people! The cloud is beginning to come down! If you've been taking unsanctified grace or unsanctified mercy and have been using it for your own gain, you must repent! If you've been saying, *I'll repent later, Lord,* or *I can get away with this and the Lord will forgive me because He's gracious and kind,* you must repent. If you have deep, hidden sins you have never confessed, repent!"

I knew unsanctified mercy would no longer be tolerated, because this cloud was bringing the holy, reverent fear of the Lord.

I shouted, "The Lord is saying, 'Come to the Mercy Seat now! The altar is open!' For if the Glory cloud hits you, I fear for your life!"

The foreboding of what was coming for those who did not repent was heavy on me. "People, if you want to get rid of those things that displease the Lord, the Mercy Seat is open today. But if you don't want to confess, if you want to stick with your secret sin, the Lord says, 'Get out of here! Run for your life!'"

> THE FOREBODING OF WHAT WAS COMING FOR THOSE WHO DID NOT REPENT WAS HEAVY ON ME.

The crowd, now seeing the cloud descending upon them, erupted into chaos. Panic ensued! People jumped out of their seats. Some leaped over rows to run to the front. Others, pushing through the crowd, ran out the back doors. Some panicked and ran to repent; others panicked and ran to escape from the Lord.

Through the bedlam I noticed bleachers at the back of the church. *Lord, what is this?* I thought. *This can't be our church. We don't have bleachers in the back.* Then I saw two well-dressed men sitting at the top of the bleachers. They hadn't moved like the rest of the crowd. They had on very smart suits, ties, and crisp white shirts. Their shoes and hair shone. They sat, legs crossed and arms folded, looking as if they were mocking. *They don't look like they belong here,* I mused. *I wonder who they are?*

Go back to them, the Lord said.

I walked toward the back. When I got within ten feet of them, they both fell off the bleachers and lay motionless on the floor. I was shocked. *Oh my gosh, Lord, are they dead? Or are they out in the Spirit?*

Never mind them, the Lord answered. *I have a word for that man at the back door.*

I crossed to the left side of the room and saw a man running back and forth from the exit door to the front and then back to the door, pausing each time before running back and forth again. When I got to him he was at the door. "Sir," I addressed him, "the Lord has a word for you. You are in secret sin with your secretary, but the Lord has had a destiny and a calling on you since you were a young man, and that calling is still there. He has not withdrawn it; He has put it on hold for you. You have followed Him, but you have been caught in a trap. If you will truly repent and go to the front, He will restore you. He will heal you, and He will bring you into your calling and your destiny. But if you walk out these church doors, I fear for your life. I fear that you are going to be turned into Lot's wife."

And I woke up.

You see, this cloud of the presence of the Lord is what we have been praying for. The cloud that descended in 1994 was quite different—full of His grace, kindness, mercy, and healing for our bodies, souls, and spirits. But the cloud that is coming carries His greatness, justice, and righteousness. It represents a dimension of His character that we have not yet seen to this extent. Most important, this cloud will carry the thing that we've been calling out for—the awesome, reverent fear of the Lord.

> THE CLOUD THAT IS
> COMING CARRIES HIS
> GREATNESS, JUSTICE,
> AND RIGHTEOUSNESS.

Father God, we want to see signs, wonders, and miracles—minds set free, cancers disappear, the deaf hear, the blind see. We want to see abortion demolished and eradicated, victims of sex trafficking rescued and healed. We want to see all these things.

But He says, *It comes with a cost; it comes with a price. Do you want more of My Glory?*

Chapter 3

THE AFTERMATH AND PRAYER

Since 1994 we have been immersed in the glorious grace, love, healing, and intimacy of Jesus our Bridegroom King, our Abba Father loving and accepting us, and the Holy Spirit guiding us in joy and intimacy with the Lord, healing our whole being—body, soul, and spirit. This encounter has given us such an appreciation and hunger for more of His presence, but we have become accustomed to His goodness, kindness, mercy, and grace, and at times we have used the grace of the Lord Jesus to get away with our own agendas, whether intentionally or not.

> AT TIMES WE HAVE USED THE GRACE OF THE LORD JESUS TO GET AWAY WITH OUR OWN AGENDAS.

HOLINESS

We are about to enter a new season, and God is extending a call to come up higher. He is sending out a warning for us to repent. We need the Holy Spirit to search our hearts and reveal known and unknown sins so we can be cleansed of them.

- ❧ Have we become too sloppy—slack about confessing our sins and allowing the Blood of Jesus to cleanse us?

- ❧ Have we become too familiar with the grace of the Lord Jesus Christ so that we are shrugging off sins thinking they are all forgiven anyway?

- ❧ Have we slipped in taking His grace and His mercy for granted and are we using it for our own convenience?

- ❧ Have we become lukewarm and lazy?

- ❧ Have we thought more highly of ourselves than we ought?

God longs to pour out a powerful anointing in these last days, but He doesn't want His children to "blow up" in the process. He doesn't want you and me to be casualties of pride, laziness, or sloppiness.

How many times has He said, "I want you to pray"? And we say, "Yes Lord, I'll do it when I get home," or He says, "I want you to phone so-and-so," and we say, "Yes Lord, I'll do it later." These seem like trivial things, but they are training wheels. They undergird the holiness into which He is calling us. It is not a holiness like religion has told us—a straitjacket of good behavior. We've gotten away with looking good on the outside while putting on a show of goodness and righteousness through our behavior, but we're rotten on the inside. Even in Jesus' day the scribes and Pharisees were rebuked for only cleaning the outside of the cup and dish, but inside they were full of greed and self-indulgence (see Matt. 23:25).

> WE'VE GOTTEN AWAY WITH
> LOOKING GOOD ON THE
> OUTSIDE WHILE PUTTING
> ON A SHOW OF GOODNESS
> AND RIGHTEOUSNESS
> THROUGH OUR BEHAVIOR.

Holiness is not performance based. It depends on a deep intimacy with Jesus our Bridegroom. That intimacy permeates every cell of our being and nourishes the fruit of holiness inside, bringing it outside to shine through our lives. It also doesn't mean that if we make a mistake, or get something wrong, He will take away His love from us. Nothing, neither:

> *Height nor depth, nor anything else in all creation, will be able to separate us from the love of God in Christ Jesus our Lord* (Romans 8:39).

He is a loving Father—a gracious Father. He is merciful. He is calling us to be like Jesus His Son. Jesus said:

> *The Son is unable to do anything from himself, or through His own initiative. I only do the works that I see the Father doing, for the Son does the same works as His Father* (John 5:19 TPT).

We read that Scripture and think of Jesus as *the Son*. We too are His children—"the son" and "the daughter." He wants us to be like Jesus—mindful and aware, asking, "Father, what are You saying? Father what are You doing?"

I don't know about you, but while I want to live like that 24/7, I am only like that at times. When I was rushing to church that Sunday and God said, "This is a test of your obedience," it really brought it home to me. It was a call to obedience.

Any test to which He subjects us is righteous and just. It is not for imposing a guilt trip.

> *Nothing I do is from my own initiative. As I hear the judgments passed by my Father, I execute those judgments. And my judgments will be perfect, because I seek only to fulfill the desires of my Father who sent me* (John 5:30 TPT).

ANY TEST TO WHICH HE SUBJECTS US IS RIGHTEOUS AND JUST. IT IS NOT FOR IMPOSING A GUILT TRIP.

You see, we are dust—we are human. Our hearts are not pure. Consciously and unconsciously, we do things that offend the Holy Spirit. We grow when we ask and allow the Holy Spirit to search our hearts and reveal anything that would hinder us from knowing our calling and

His anointing upon us. That is the antidote to apathy and indifference toward the Holy Spirit. It doesn't mean you won't have wonderful, raucous times with the Lord in joy, laughter, and freedom. We have to know our relationship with Him is more than that. It also involves obedience and the awesome, reverential fear of the Lord.

Could something in your life be hindering you from a more intimate walk with the Lord? Let's find out now and deal with our issues today. Take a moment and ask the Holy Spirit:

> *Holy Spirit, is there anything in my heart and in my life that displeases the Father and Jesus? I don't want to keep it. I want to come to Your Mercy Seat right now.*

If He says anything or something comes to mind, please don't ignore it or stuff it down. Deal with it. He is giving you an opportunity for freedom, forgiveness, and a new impartation—a calling to go higher.

A PASSIONATE BRIDE

Every year John and I teach at the School of Ministry. On one particular occasion, when I had been teaching on the soon coming of the Lord, He gave me a prophetic word that caused me to shake physically. I knew this was for more than just that moment:

> You, who have ears to hear Me, I am talking to you right now. I have been talking to you, and you have not been listening.
>
> I want you hot!
>
> I want you hot!
>
> I want you hot!
>
> I want you passionate—whole hearted.
>
> My Son paid a big price. He went to the cross for a Bride that loves Him—for a

Bride that adores Him—and I will not give Him anything less.

I am calling you!

I am calling you right now to lay down those things—those big things, those little things, and those things I abhor—those things you think you have been getting away with, thinking no one is watching and no one is seeing. But I am watching and I am seeing and I will not allow it anymore in these days, because My Son is coming for a Bride who is without spot and without wrinkle—one that only has eyes for My Son. I will not have a Bride that has eyes for other things—for the things of the world, for the things of the ministry. I will only come for a Bride who has eyes for My Son and who loves Him with an incredible passion.

I WILL ONLY COME FOR
A BRIDE WHO HAS EYES
FOR MY SON AND WHO
LOVES HIM WITH AN
INCREDIBLE PASSION.

I am a God of passion. My name is *Love* and I will not have a Bride that is anything less than filled with passion, filled with love, and filled with adoration for My Son. The hour is short, and I am giving you a chance right now to turn from your wicked ways—to turn from your lukewarm ways and ask the Lord of passion, the Lord of love, to rekindle and set ablaze those areas in your heart. You see, I will answer, just like I will with anyone who would say, "There's a part in my heart, Lord, that is not fully yielded to You."

The Lord would say, I see those areas in your heart, and some of you don't even know how to get ignited again, but I do. If you ask Me and are really serious and are really wanting Me to change you, I will come and I will heal and I will restore those areas in your heart and I will put that passion and that flame in your heart for My Son, because I am a Father who really loves you. If I did not love you, I would not give you this warning. He would just come suddenly, and you would not know. But I am your loving Father and I do really love you. I really care for you and I want you in the Body. I want you in the Bride—passionate and in love with My Son.

Be careful that you never allow your hearts to grow cold. Be careful that you are not caught off guard, or your hearts will be weighed down with carousing, drunkenness, and the worries of this life, and that day will come upon you suddenly like a trap. Don't let me come and find you drunk or living carelessly like everyone else. For that day will come as a shocking surprise to all (Luke 21:34-35 TPT).

God, I invite your searching gaze into my heart. Examine me through and through; find out everything that may be hidden within me. Put me to the test and sift through all my anxious cares. See if there is any path of pain I'm walking on, and lead me back to your glorious, everlasting way—the path that brings me back to you (Psalm 139:23-24 TPT).

Some of us have prayed Psalm 139 many times, and for some of us this is the first time we are sincerely surrendering our hearts to be honest, vulnerable, and examined through and through by the Holy Spirit.

> *Holy Spirit, I want Your conviction in my life.*
>
> *Heavenly Father, I so thank You for Your love and Your awesome grace and mercy.*
>
> *I repent today for taking Your mercy and Your grace for granted. Lord, I repent and I give You permission to remind me quickly when I do something that displeases You.*
>
> *I want to be a child who hears Your voice and obeys You. Lord, I repent, I turn away from all sin, I bring any secret sin to the light. I repent of any sexual sin, lustful thoughts, jealousy and envy, comparison, lying, anger.*
>
> *I forgive those who have hurt and wounded me, and I forgive myself for the mistakes I've made.*

And Father, if I have judged You for when I've felt abandoned or hurt, or for not preventing painful situations, I repent for blaming You. Lord, whatever it is You are putting Your finger on that is hidden or not, I surrender to You. Lord, I want clean hands and a pure heart.

I want to hear You and obey. I no longer want anything unclean or sinful in my life. I desire to walk with You, because Lord You are love, but You are also power. You want me to be able to walk not only in Your love, but to be trusted with Your power to heal the sick, to set the captives free.

Lord, You want the lost to come in, not only in church but on the streets. Thank You, Jesus, for Your forgiveness that removes all shame, all hindrances, so that wherever I am I can walk in Your anointing and Your love and give it away. Thank You, Jesus. Amen.

A Spotless Bride

He who has prepared us for this very thing is God, who has given us the Spirit as a guarantee (2 Corinthians 5:5).

Is it possible for us to be pure before the Lord? Can we truly be free from *every* spot and wrinkle of sin that has tainted us? What do we do to become a "spotless Bride," and how do we do it?

None of us has lived a perfect life. We all need cleansing and healing to the degree that life has brought difficult circumstances our way. For me, asking God to examine my heart over and over has been an ongoing process. Even in the past couple of years I've gone deeper into my healing journey than I ever thought possible.

We need to be kind to ourselves. It took us years to get to where we are today. Healing needs time, and the Lord is very patient. He looks at our hearts to see our willingness to surrender. Sometimes there are seasons when we feel like we need to dig something up and get it healed, but God has a process. He is patiently carrying us along, and in His timing He brings full healing. That timing depends on our humility, surrender, and vulnerability.

Sometimes in the healing process, it is hard to walk through painful places on our own even though the Lord is with us every step of the way. The good news is, we don't have to do it alone! I have had many, many individuals walk alongside me in my healing journey. There is power in walking together with each other in the light of God's Word. Together we strengthen, empower, and encourage each other as God works through us.

> *Therefore confess your sins to each other and pray for each other so that you may be healed. The prayer of a righteous man is powerful and effective* (James 5:16 NIV).

> ### THERE IS POWER IN WALKING TOGETHER WITH EACH OTHER IN THE LIGHT OF GOD'S WORD.

Not only do we benefit in life and in our relationships with others when we receive healing from the Lord, but Scripture tells us we are to take the spots and wrinkles out of our wedding gown to be ready for the wedding celebration of the Lamb, our Lord Jesus Christ:

> *Let us rejoice and exalt Him and give him glory, because the wedding celebration of the Lamb has come. And His Bride has made herself ready* (Revelation 19:7 TPT).

The place of being submitted to the process of repentance for our sins as God reveals our "spots and wrinkles" is such a beautiful, safe place to be.

It is the place of abiding in Him. In that place we are surrendered, humble, teachable, and sensitive to the Holy Spirit's voice to correct, guide, lead, and love us. When we abide in Him, we don't miss out on anything the Father wants to do in us, with us, and through us.

Our Father is never a "respecter of persons" (see Acts 10:34). Whether we are a leader of many or just starting our own healing journey, the journey never ends. God the Father is always calling us higher. It never gets boring, and there is no time to get lazy! He works with us steadily and diligently so we can become the Bride (see Rev. 19:7)—one who has *made herself ready and is without spot or wrinkle.*

Chapter 4

VISION OF THE BRIDE

In 1994, when we were just three weeks into the glorious outpouring of the Holy Spirit with manifestations of God's presence all around us, John and I had to leave on a mission trip. Many questions came to our minds: How could we possibly go to Hungary with the revival of a lifetime happening at our church? And if we left, would the Holy Spirit still keep coming? We didn't want to go. We were really in a dilemma, yet prior to the revival breaking out we had made a commitment to go to Hungary. Try as we might to postpone the trip for a later date, it was not possible, since the organizers had fully planned and advertised their event. In the end we resigned ourselves to going and had our team pray for us to send us off with God's blessing.

As they were praying, I suddenly fell to the floor under the power of the Holy Spirit and was instantly in the most incredible Technicolor vision of my entire life.

Never before had I experienced a vision! I say that with utmost sincerity. I had *never* had a vision! If someone asked me to picture my house in my head, I would just draw a blank. I literally *could not* "picture" in my head. I could describe something I had seen from memory, but I couldn't see it. Not only that, but the vision lasted about 45 minutes—the entire time speaker Marc Dupont was preaching. It was stunning and unbelievable to be in a full color vision that appeared entirely like reality!

Just to give you a visual from John's and the congregation's perspective, all they could see was a woman lying on her back on the platform, sometimes with her legs straight up in the air "running," arms flying, reaching up. All of this activity was happening right near the podium where our dear friend Marc was trying to preach.

I was such a distraction, as you can imagine, that ushers and others approached John asking, "Should we move Carol off to the side?"

"Nobody touch her," John instructed firmly. "She would never do anything like this. Not even for a million dollars. God is doing something powerful in her."

So I stayed there.

I'm not sure how much of the sermon anyone heard, but I was having a marvelous time with Jesus!

I'M NOT SURE HOW MUCH OF THE SERMON ANYONE HEARD, BUT I WAS HAVING A MARVELOUS TIME WITH JESUS!

THE VISION

When I went into the vision, I suddenly found myself in a beautiful meadow. Jesus walked up to me and handed me a bouquet of lilies of the valley.

There is a story to the significance of that bouquet.

In the spring of 1978, John and I had met in a nearby city to have dinner (we were just acquaintances at that time), and his mother had sent along a bouquet of lilies of the valley for me. After dinner John headed back to Toronto and I headed home to Stratford. I had set the flowers on the passenger seat for the drive home. I was feeling very overwhelmed because I had recently been divorced. I was very heavy in my spirit, since I was a single mom with two young boys. Even as I sat in the car I was crying out to the Lord from the depth of my heart, *Oh God! Oh Jesus, where are You in all this? What do I do? As a Christian woman how do I navigate my life now?*

Tears streaming down my face, I poured out my heart and frustrations to Jesus.

Suddenly a fragrance filled the car, the clouds above parted, and sunbeams radiated around me touching the earth and reaching into the car. In wonder I picked up the bouquet of lilies of the valley from the front seat, and as I did the Lord spoke to me. *Carol, lilies of the valley do not grow on mountain tops. They only grow in valleys, and whenever you are in a valley I will always have My lilies there for you.*

> SUDDENLY A FRAGRANCE
> FILLED THE CAR, THE
> CLOUDS ABOVE PARTED,
> AND SUNBEAMS RADIATED
> AROUND ME.

The lilies signified His presence, His light, His compassion, His care, and His overwhelming love and concern for every detail of my life.

As Jesus handed the bouquet to me, I knew exactly what He meant. We spent the next while, which seemed like a long time, laughing and talking about all the things that happened during my life. We ran, held hands, and danced in circles, enjoying every moment together.

Then He asked me for the bouquet back. You know girls don't like to give bouquets back, so I felt a little sad, but I gave it back. Jesus walked around picking all different colors of flowers—red, yellow, purple, blue, white—and began weaving them into a wreath. He inserted the lilies of the valley into the wreath and placed it on my head. Out of nowhere came a long, white wedding veil that He attached to the back of the wreath.

The scene changed, and I found myself walking arm in arm with Jesus in an entirely different place. People were lined up along the street waving, cheering, and looking very happy. As I wondered where I was and who these people were, I suddenly noticed *what was under my feet*. I was shocked! The street was made of *gold!*

Oh my goodness, I thought, *I am in Heaven!*

I was walking with Jesus on the streets of gold! "I am marrying Jesus!" I cried out. As soon as I uttered the words, the scene changed again.

This time I found myself in a massive banquet hall, Jesus seemingly behind me. From where I was looking, as far as the eye could see, there were tables fully set. They looked beautiful with flowers, china, cutlery, glasses. Everything looked perfect; everything looked ready, but the gigantic hall was empty. No one was there.

"Where are all the people?" I asked Jesus.

At that moment I felt to look behind me and I saw the most beautiful people! Their faces were shining. They were smiling and absolutely radiant. They were dressed in the most exquisite wedding attire—a stunning sight.

"Jesus," I breathed, "who are these people?"

"They are the broken, the hurting, the outcast, and the downtrodden—the ones nobody loves and nobody cares for. I have bidden them to come to My banquet feast."

I COULDN'T BELIEVE HOW BEAUTIFUL AND RADIANT THE PEOPLE WERE.

My heart was in awe. I couldn't believe how beautiful and radiant the people were. Beaming smiles, eyes sparking, everyone looked so incredibly happy, expectant, and excited. They were so full of light and life.

At that point Jesus reached out to me and asked me for the first dance. The moment was very meaningful to me.

When I first received Jesus as my personal Lord and Savior, I read in the Bible that we would get a crown. At that time I asked the Lord if, whenever I went to Heaven, I could just have a great big, long hug from Him as a reward instead

of that crown. As a new believer I didn't understand the significance of the crown, and as a single
mom I just needed a good, long hug. Thus, when
Jesus asked for the first dance and hugged me
close, I knew it was an answer to that prayer of
long ago. As we began to dance, I realized that
my wedding veil was too long for dancing. It was
just a thought, but immediately, out of nowhere
came birds—little sparrows, cardinals, blue jays,
and others. They picked up my wedding veil, and
I danced with Jesus.

So Come

*I awoke from the vision at the end of the service. Some
ministry was still happening, and most people were
still there. The presence of Jesus was still so intense
around me. I basked in it, trying to comprehend where
I had just been and what I had seen and heard. John
must have noticed I had settled and was no longer
running in the air or making unusual movements. He*

came to me and asked if I was still in the vision or if I could share what had happened to me with the people.

Lord, I asked, *can I share the vision and what do You want me to say?*

He told me to have our worship leader sing Kevin Prosch's song, "So Come."

SO COME

You have taken the precious
From the worthless and given us
Beauty for ashes, love for hate.
You have chosen the weak things
Of the world to shame that which
is strong,
And foolish things to shame the wise.
You are help to the helpless,
Strength to the strengthless,

And a father to the child who's left alone.

And the thirsty You've invited

To come drink the water

And those who have no money come and buy.

Chorus: So come! So come!

Behold the days are coming

For the Lord has promised

That the plowman will overtake the reaper.

And our hearts will be the threshing floor

And the move of God we've cried out for

Will come, it will surely come.

For You will shake the heavens,

And fill your house with Glory,

And turn the shame of outcasts into praise.

All creation groans and waits

For the Spirit and the Bride to say

The words that your heart had longed to hear.

After the song Jesus told me to tell the people, *The banquet feast is almost ready.*

I shared the full vision, and as I finished I heard the Lord tell me to say to the people that they are to be like the five wise virgins in Matthew 25. Then I taught on the parable of the virgins.

WISE OR FOOLISH

The story in Matthew 25 is about ten virgins. All ten had lit their lamps, and all were waiting for the Bridegroom to come, yet the Bridegroom was delayed. As a result, all ten fell sound asleep. Suddenly a cry came at midnight:

Behold the Bridegroom is coming!

All ten virgins woke up and trimmed their lamps, but a problem arose. Five said to the other five:

Give us some of your oil.

Our lamps ran out of oil and we didn't bring extra.

The five who had not brought extra oil were foolish. The five wise virgins who had extra oil said:

No! Go and buy for yourselves.

While they were gone, Jesus the Bridegroom came and invited the five wise ones into the wedding feast and shut the door behind them. When the five foolish returned, they knocked on the banquet door. Jesus opened it to them and said:

I never knew you.

The word *knew* means to know someone intimately, as opposed to knowing about someone.

The Lord said to me to tell the people, *This is a time that I am pouring out extra oil. Buy oil!*

THE COST OF INTIMACY IS VULNERABILITY AND HUMILITY.

The cost of intimacy is vulnerability and humility. The oil is the Holy Spirit who ignites intimacy with Jesus in us in our relationship with Jesus. No one else can give us some of their intimacy with Jesus. Just like in any other special relationship, as you spend time with that person and cultivate intimacy, your relationship develops and grows.

After I had that vision, I asked the Lord, *What kind of wedding dress will the Bride wear?*

He responded, *My Bride will be clothed in My Glory.*

When the Glory cloud comes, we'll be His Bride without spot or wrinkle, ready to wear His Glory.

This vision and word stirred John to study Matthew 25 over and over and over again. He learned the importance of Prophetic Symbolism. Then, one day as John was studying, the Lord spoke to him:

If you would have stopped Carol that night, your revival would have only lasted about three weeks.

John was stunned. "Wow! What? Why?"

I was painting a prophetic picture on her heart of what I wanted to do in Toronto and the world, the Lord said. Toronto Airport Church was to become a place where people could come to buy the oil of intimacy.

Oh! How important our obedience is!

How important it is to hear His voice and act on it!

And how important it is that we invest into our relationship with the Lord and take the time to cultivate our intimacy with Him!

No one can do that for us. No one can give us the oil of intimacy. We must go and buy it for ourselves.

> NO ONE CAN GIVE US
> THE OIL OF INTIMACY.
> WE MUST GO AND BUY
> IT FOR OURSELVES.

Just like He did in Toronto, God sets up places for the outpouring of His Spirit so we can go there to encounter Jesus, be equipped, be healed, and be set free from barriers and hindrances. These places are one way that God provides for us to "buy oil." Yet the core of our relationship—our daily walk and communion with Him—is our main way of "buying oil." In His love and generosity, through these two ways He pours out His Holy Spirit on us, blesses us, and immerses us in His presence. Both experiences are precious and powerful moments in history when Heaven touches earth. They provide acceleration into the heart of the Father and a time to be filled with the precious oil of intimacy.

Chapter 5

BE WISE AND BUY OIL

That wonderful, foundational vision moved and awakened in John and me the expectation and urgency of the soon return of the Lord Jesus. Since that time we keep hearing the cry: *Are you ready?*

The Bridegroom is coming!

The Bridegroom is coming!

Go out to meet Him.

The "oil" the wise virgins carried refers to a life full of the Holy Spirit and on fire for God. The oil, or Holy Spirit, is the fuel that ignites the fire in us like the oil that fueled the lamps of the virgins. We've tried to be faithful to that vision, and the Lord graciously allowed us to become an "oil dispensing station" in Toronto. The nations came and are still coming and buying the oil of intimacy. You, possibly, bought fresh oil in Toronto yourself! What did this incredible refilling of the Holy Spirit do in you and in the tens of thousands of others who came to be filled?

THE HOLY SPIRIT IS THE FUEL
THAT IGNITES THE FIRE IN US.

Suddenly our souls and our passion for Jesus burst into flame and we were alive again in the Spirit! It was the most transforming and awe-inspiring experience of our lives. We have told people over and over, "Don't get tired of coming and buying oil again and again. Be sure you carry a large reserve supply."

FLOOR TIME

When people are touched by the power of God through the Holy Spirit, often they lose physical strength and fall to the floor just like I did when I received prayer on the platform. The moments of resting on the floor are rich with the enveloping embrace of God's presence as He works in us for good. We call this "floor time" or "soaking." When people fell to the floor during meetings in the early days of the revival in Toronto, I would tell them, "Don't let anyone discourage you from taking time to soak in His presence. Wait and listen to the Lord while you lie on the floor loving Jesus and being filled by Him."

MARY AND MARTHA

John and I have taught about Mary and Martha and encouraged people to be like Mary who loved Him and wanted only to sit at His feet and hear His words. Martha was "concerned about many things" and didn't take the opportunity to rest in Jesus' presence as did her sister. The caution to us is not to operate like Martha and become one of those described in Matthew 22:1-9, who were too busy when the Bridegroom invited them to attend the wedding feast.

> PEOPLE WHO ARE LIKE MARY,
> FULL OF THE HOLY SPIRIT,
> CAN OUT-PERFORM OTHERS
> IN MINISTRY AND SERVICE
> ANY DAY OF THE WEEK.

Is it worth being that busy? With our busyness are we achieving a lot more than if we spent some of that time with Jesus? I am convinced that people who are like Mary, full of the Holy Spirit, can out-perform others in ministry and service any day of the week. Some may be concerned that spending time with God can spin one's life out of control to where all one does is "soak" rather than accomplish any "real" work. I've never seen it go that way. Rather, I see people fall passionately in love with Jesus, be filled with the oil God is pouring out, and take off in ministry with fire and zeal unlike anything they have done before.

BUY NOW

When do you buy oil? Now is the time.

All ten virgins expected the return of the Bridegroom.

All ten had burning lamps.

All ten fell asleep while waiting for the Bridegroom to return.

All ten woke up when they heard the cry—the Bridegroom is coming!

What was the difference? The five wise had *extra* oil—the oil of intimacy.

The virgins are types of Christians. They all represent the Church, but the five wise represent the Church that intimately knows Jesus.

At the time I had the vision years ago, John was studying Matthew 25, but as he read it, he sensed it was a very sobering passage. He began to understand what it says—the Lord is coming for His Bride, and His Bride, according to this passage, is actually quite ready and waiting for Him. But let's be clear: *five virgins (believers) got to go somewhere where the other five virgins (believers) did not get to go!*

Where did the five wise go? They went to the wedding!

What happened to the other five? They got set aside.

Why? Because they had run out of oil!

We *need* to know about this oil, because this is a wedding story. It concerns the oil of intimacy and relationship with the Son of God who is seeking His Bride.

John likes digging into the Greek and Hebrew. He researched the words in the passage. Some powerful and shaking revelations emerged. Suddenly it took on new life because its meaning became so much clearer.

When Jesus says to the five foolish ones, "I never *knew* you," Scripture uses the Greek word *oida,* which means "to see and behold, perceive, be intimately acquainted with, appreciate." He does not use the word *gnosko,* which means I knew *about* you—I knew where you lived, I had information concerning you, or I had some intellectual knowledge about you. That's not the word used. He used the word *oida,* which means to know *intimately*—to look into one's eyes, connect with one's heart. When He says, "I never knew you," He is saying, *I never knew you intimately. I never connected with your heart.*

SOON

As John read and reread this passage, he became aware of the words, "while the Bridegroom was delayed, they all slumbered and slept." He stopped right there and said to God, "I don't feel like I'm asleep. I feel like I'm more wide awake than I've ever been in all my life. We've got thousands of people coming to our church. People are getting saved, healed, and powerfully touched by the Holy Spirit. It's amazing, Lord! I love it! I feel more wide awake than I have ever been!"

In a flash God retorted, *You are asleep concerning the message of the soon return of the Lord Jesus Christ!*

It struck hard.

The words pierced John's spirit, cut right through him, and he realized that we had not preached the precious message of Jesus' return for at least ten years. Why not? We had to assess our thoughts.

The tactics of the enemy to influence us are very subtle. John was *turned off* the message! Can you think of *why* he was turned off? He was turned off for the very reason that so many others were turned off—at one point it was quite the trending thing to predict the date Jesus would return. Someone you know will remember the book about the 88 reasons why Jesus was coming back in '88. Too many self-appointed prophets were setting dates and being proved wrong. Christians were getting their hopes up thinking, *Maybe this time,* and then were let down. Nothing. Nothing again. Nothing yet again.

John stopped preaching about it.

We didn't know at that time how the Lord wanted us to relate to His message concerning Jesus' return. Now we understand He was calling us to *live in tension*. He wants us to hold on to two truths:

- perhaps today
- perhaps in 100 years

Jesus may return today, or we may get to live out all our years on earth before He returns. It's all good. Are we to predict the date of His coming? No. Scripture teaches we will know the season, but not the day or the hour. Three key points help indicate we are nearing the season of His return:

- Israel is a nation.
- Jerusalem is her capital.
- The Gospel has gone to the nations.

SCRIPTURE TEACHES WE WILL KNOW THE SEASON, BUT NOT THE DAY OR THE HOUR.

John's new book, *The Promise of His Coming,* goes into these key points in greater detail. You will find it very encouraging and helpful.

We will also look to Matthew 24 where Jesus outlines a few more clues for us. From these signs we can assess that we are in the season.

DON'T MISS THE BOAT

Around the time God awakened us to His message of Jesus' soon return, John had a dream that brought greater insight into the parable of the wise virgins, framing it in a context that is perhaps easier to visualize.

In the dream John and I were about to go on a cruise ship. John told me to board while he checked the departure time to make sure our tickets were in order. He then headed back to the ship when, to his amazement, he heard the drone of the ship's horn as it sailed away.

His first thought was, *Oh Lord! I've missed the boat!*

His second thought was, *Oh no! Carol is on the boat!*

For the rest of dream he was ploughing through difficulties, trying to find the next port of call so he could get on the boat, join me, and be part of the cruise.

THE MAIN MESSAGE

The message of the dream is clear. The Lord is saying, Don't miss the boat!

John missed the boat not because he did something he ought not be doing. He missed it just because he was doing "life" and going about his business. Is God warning that we could miss the return of the Lord for His Bride for very simple and mundane reasons? Scripture gives us some insights.

DON'T MISS THE BOAT!

In Matthew 24 Jesus explains that He is coming as a thief in the night. No man knows the day or the hour. Not even Jesus. Only the Father knows when He is sending His Son to get His Bride. Sincere believers may be thinking:

- We've got lots of time.

- I don't see any changes that indicate Jesus is coming soon.

- I think other stuff has to happen first before He comes back.

- Jesus' coming for His Bride is not as important as seeing people saved.

Interestingly, the last point is most important. Many believe that God's top priority is for us to win the lost and bring in the harvest, but I tell you with assurance that is not so. The main message is:

Be ready.

Fall in love.

Buy oil.

Let me walk you through and show you.

When we nurture our intimacy with Jesus as our priority, we are filled with oil. *All* other things, all of which are very important, flow naturally, without striving, from a heart of love.

ALL OTHER THINGS
FLOW NATURALLY FROM
A HEART OF LOVE.

A heart of love beats in one who has fallen in love. Are you in love with Him? Is it your heart's deepest desire to please Him, to be humble and vulnerable, so that you can truly say before Heaven and earth, "Lord, I love You with all my heart, soul, and mind" (see Matt. 22:37)?

I believe that you, just as much as I, want to say when you meet Jesus, "I wasn't just *working* for You; I wasn't just a good martyr trying to buy Your favor. Lord, I am absolutely *in love* with You!"

> LOVE THE LORD YOUR GOD WITH ALL YOUR HEART, SOUL, AND MIND SO THAT THE DATE DOES NOT COME UPON YOU UNAWARE.

Before I obey God's command to love my neighbor as myself, and before I plant churches for Him or help pastors and disciple them, I have to take care of the very first order of business: *Love the Lord your God with all your heart, soul, and mind so that the date does not come upon you unaware.* That is the first and most important commandment (see Deut. 6:5).

John and I have watched as the Holy Spirit has taken the spots and wrinkles out of our wedding dress and that of untold numbers of others throughout the years (see Rev. 19:7-9). We have seen deep wounds, fears, angers, rejections, and every kind of hurt brought into the light of His love. We have listened to testimony after testimony of the incredible healing our Bridegroom has imparted to the heart of His Bride. She is adorning herself with jewels of humility and obedience. She is anointing herself with the sweet perfume of the Holy Spirit. Love and mercy are her crown. These are the things the Lord loves.

MINISTER FROM THE OVERFLOW

We continually need to buy oil, because we do not know the day or the hour. Our pursuit of intimacy never stops, but out of that intimacy, and out of our heart of love for Jesus, we also respond to His call to minister—pour out to the lost and hurting, heal the sick, bind up the brokenhearted, set the captives free, and preach the good news of His Kingdom and salvation. Ministry that touches and transforms lives needs oil! It's our fuel—the Holy Spirit's anointing.

MINISTRY THAT TOUCHES AND TRANSFORMS LIVES NEEDS OIL!

The power of the Holy to Spirit helps us fulfill the great commandment to love the Lord our God with all our heart and soul, to love our neighbors, and to make disciples. This oil fuels our relationship with Him and keeps the fire burning in our hearts so that on the great day when we hear the cry, "The Bridegroom is coming," we can meet Him confidently, knowing we are filled with oil, look into His eyes, and hear Him say, "I *know* you. Come into the wedding feast."

Chapter 6

HOLY SPIRIT
TRANSFORMATION

The Bible begins and ends with marriage. Everything in between is intended to prepare us to be a passionate Bride without spot or wrinkle—one who walks on Earth doing the things her Bridegroom did, and even greater things than those (see John 14:12). We are meant to walk in that kind of power and fruitfulness, and it must flow out of intimacy and rest rather than achievement, good works, and striving.

Our focus, therefore, is not power, but rather the cultivation of an intimate relationship with Jesus, our Bridegroom King. Our relationship with Him motivates us to love others, serve others, and lay down our lives for others, because our service springs out of our love for Him, not out of a longing for His approval.

> OUR SERVICE SPRINGS OUT
> OF OUR LOVE FOR HIM,
> NOT OUT OF A LONGING
> FOR HIS APPROVAL.

You have been chosen by the King of Glory and appointed to bear lovely fruit with incredible fruitfulness!

> *Lord, come and clothe Your Bride with Your Glory, for we have come to seek Your face and draw near. We are desperate to know You more.*

OUR COMFORTER, OUR HELPER

What are we going to do now? He is gone!

The hearts of the disciples were shattered with grief when Jesus died on the Cross—until they remembered His words of promise, comfort, and peace. What was the promise that transformed them and the world?

> *These things I have spoken to you while I am still with you. But the Helper, the Holy Spirit, whom the Father will send in my name, he will teach you all things*

and bring to your remembrance all that I have said to you (John 14:25-26).

We are not meant to do life as believers all on our own. We have the Holy Spirit to help us. A transformation takes place when we surrender and commit our lives to Jesus. One of the best analogies is that of a butterfly.

When a caterpillar forms the chrysalis, it actually liquefies, and pieces are moved around in patterns in order to form a new creation. A butterfly is quite literally a whole new, beautiful creation. The same is true of us. When we are born again, all the old is melted away and we are transformed and reborn:

> *Therefore, if anyone is in Christ, he is a new creation. The old has passed away; behold, the new has come* (2 Corinthians 5:17).

That is a transformation. It is defined as a change in form, appearance, nature, or character.

It is a conversion, metamorphosis, or transfiguration. In us, transformation is only possible by the power of the Holy Spirit. To work with us, He requires our vulnerability and humility.

> TO WORK WITH US, HE
> REQUIRES OUR VULNERABILITY
> AND HUMILITY.

The illustration of the butterfly is meaningful to me personally. One afternoon while I was in my backyard praying about transformation, I saw a beautiful monarch butterfly. The Lord reminded me how its life began.

The butterfly started out as a little egg that hatched into a caterpillar (in my opinion, not a very nice-looking one). That little caterpillar didn't know the incredible process the Lord had planned for it—a metamorphosis, a change in form, appearance, nature, and character from a worm into a magnificent, glistening creature with so much intelligence that it can fly to Mexico to the exact same tree and return. The migration takes multiple generations. Each butterfly lives only for one month, but it takes three months for that tiny creature to fly from Mexico to Canada. What incredible design! In total it takes six generations of monarch butterflies to do a round trip of migration. Wow! What a God we have to have envisioned a plan like that!

CHANGE IS COMING

It seems transformation is upon us. Many of us are sensing a major shift coming in each of us personally and in the Body of Christ worldwide. In fact, it is already in process. We are coming into a "chrysalis" season. What does that mean?

Here is a picture of what God did in my life, and probably in yours as well.

Transformation is Upon Us.

From the time we are born, we are all on a journey along rocky paths in a wilderness of sin, pain, and hurt in search of something better. Then, possibly through a fellow traveler who extended a hand to lift us up when we were down, we found Jesus! His touch revived us and filled us up with love, light, and hope. We were "born again." Suddenly the sky looked bluer, the grass greener, and our hearts began to soar as transformation took root.

Let's look at the wonderful process Jesus takes us through.

Some of us may feel stuck and dry, while others are on fire and excited to see what God is about to do. I want you to remember that little worm in the chrysalis. Let's turn back and look at our roots. Where did we come from? Do we need to revisit some of the painful areas that we have tried to forget?

Sometimes we get really impatient with the process as it is seems to take too long. We may have received prophetic words that were wonderful, but that was a long time ago. None of them have come to pass yet. Maybe it was so long ago you can't even recall those prophetic words or any words of encouragement spoken to you.

If that little worm was a thinking being, I'm sure it was wondering, *What on earth is happening to me?* Isn't it true that sometimes we feel like our lives are "melting" around us and being rearranged, and there's nothing we can do about it except to remember that our heavenly Father has a wonderful plan and destiny for us?

A PLAN AND DESTINY

The Book of Esther tells the story of a little orphan girl raised by her uncle Mordecai. He had the brilliant idea that she should enter the king's beauty pageant because he wanted to select a new queen. The king had issued a proclamation in the land to all beautiful young virgins in his kingdom to apply. I so admire Esther for her obedience to her uncle and her willingness to say yes, considering the overwhelming changes to which she might be required to submit.

Suddenly, without knowing the outcome, this little Jewish girl was taken from all that was familiar to her and immersed into the lifestyle of a pagan palace to be transformed. Her transformation, or process, required disciplined and intense beauty treatments for a year. But she wasn't alone. Her heavenly Father gave her wisdom as she and her maids prayed faithfully. He also granted her favor not only in the sight of the eunuch—the custodian of the women—but also in the eyes of all who encountered her.

Eventually the day came when she was to present herself before King Ahasuerus. What was the outcome? He loved Esther over all the other women and she obtained grace and favor in his sight. The young Jewish girl became the queen instead of Vashti, because God had a plan.

TIME WITH THE KING

One of the ways I prepare myself for our Bridegroom King is by spending quality time with Him. I don't go to Him with an agenda or a prayer list. I just go to enjoy being with Him. I position myself and my heart for intimacy. That's what I call soaking. "Be still, and know that I am God" (Ps. 46:10).

How often do we remember just to be quiet and let Him do some of the talking? That's what soaking is all about. (See the Appendix for an introduction to soaking.)

> HOW OFTEN DO WE REMEMBER JUST TO BE QUIET AND LET HIM DO SOME OF THE TALKING?

If you have soaked, you know how wonderful it is to come to Jesus in the quiet, with no agenda, and listen for His still, small voice—literally just to soak, even marinate, in His presence. Instrumental worship music can provide a peaceful background for taking time to rest with Him.

Through soaking, or spending time in His presence without an agenda, the reality of God is present, powerful, intimate, and life-changing.

I have been dramatically transformed through soaking. Years ago He said to me, *Carol, I have many servants, but few lovers—lots of Marthas, few Marys.* Then we learned about the five wise virgins and the coming Glory. I desperately wanted to be incredibly close to my Savior, absolutely transformed into a wise virgin waiting for her Bridegroom. Soaking is a vital part of my journey to be a Mary, not just a Martha.

One of the most important things the Lord said to me in a time of soaking was, *Sell me the most valuable thing that you own.*

I was puzzled. "What do You mean, Lord? Sell my house? I'll have to ask John since he owns half. The only other sort of valuable thing is my horse. Lord, do You want me to sell my horse? I don't understand. What are You asking, Lord?"

Carol, he said, *the most valuable thing you own is your* time. *Sell Me your* time *and buy the pearl of great price, which is intimacy with Jesus.*

At first I didn't realize I was "soaking." A girl friend of mine in England and I would just be praying, worshiping, and resting in the presence of God when we began to notice an increase of His presence and His anointing.

Then soaking really took on a new dimension in the revival services in 1995. A few things happened that converged, bringing us a bigger picture of soaking. I'll explain a few here.

First, I used to sit beside people who were lying on the floor, praying over them to keep them there. I later learned that it was very similar to what Francis and Judith McNutt were known to do in their soaking/healing ministry. I encouraged people to remain on the floor as I poured prayer into them for hours. I didn't realize at the time that I was "soaking" them.

I started to do this because I noticed that if someone wasn't with another person, after they received prayed and were lying on the floor, they would feel nervous and self-conscious and would get up. But if someone was there praying over them, allowing the anointing to flow through and fill them, they would continue to rest in God's presence and their lives would never be the same again.

Second, during the revival I was often on the floor in His presence myself. In my own experience, when I was first filled with the Spirit as a new Christian, I put on worship music and just immersed myself in Him. I didn't know that was soaking. I felt I was just spending time with Him. Then He began speaking to me. Often during worship in the revival, I lay down, put my head under my chair so I wouldn't be distracted or interrupted, and let the Holy Spirit fill me. I noticed His presence got stronger and His anointing thicker while I was lying there.

> ## LIVES, CHURCHES, AND ENTIRE REGIONS WERE BEING CHANGED.

Third, the testimonies! Testimonies people gave after soaking during floor time, or "carpet time," were just incredible. They were having amazing visions (myself included) and being healed, set free, and filled with the fire of the Holy Spirit. Lives, churches, and entire regions were being changed.

Finally, at our School of Ministry, we have always encouraged students just to lie before the Lord, to try not to pray and explain themselves but let Him speak, and to give Jesus space to come and be with them, and them with Him. This is a two-way love affair with Jesus. It is not an intercession time.

All these things together began forming our value in soaking. Soaking teachings, soaking centers, and books on soaking followed. That's the beautiful thing when you spend time with Jesus— good fruit comes out of it!

Learning to soak doesn't always happen instantaneously. It takes practice to set aside the busyness of your mind and your life and allow the Holy Spirit to come and speak. It is a process, and in that process we learn that prayer is only part of our relationship with Jesus. In prayer we share our needs with Him. He wants us to pray, but during soaking we go before Him with no agenda—no list of requests for Him to review. Can you imagine if we only spent time with our loved ones to tell them all the things we needed them to do for us and everything that was upsetting us? It would be difficult to enjoy relationships like that. We need to have time with Jesus to get to *know Him* and have a relationship—a love affair.

> WE NEED TO HAVE TIME WITH JESUS TO GET TO KNOW HIM AND HAVE A RELATIONSHIP—A LOVE AFFAIR.

Scripture tells us, *"Be still, and know that I am God"* (Ps. 46:10). Is that ever true! My book *Soaking in the Spirit* is a wonderful resource to start your soaking journey. A journal that walks you through the process of soaking supplements it. Both are available on Amazon.

We soaked all the time at our church and emphasized our soaking centers and soaking nights. We placed great value on the time we spent soaking, yet I have noticed lately that soaking in general is losing its place of esteem. It isn't happening as often as it used to individually, and especially on a church-wide basis. Sometimes we don't need to look for the next, new "big thing" to come along. Often we just need to slow down, quiet ourselves before Him, return to the Psalms, and let Him transform us. He is always calling us deeper into His Word, into intimacy, and into a consecrated inner holiness.

> HE IS ALWAYS CALLING US
> DEEPER INTO HIS WORD,
> INTO INTIMACY, AND
> INTO A CONSECRATED
> INNER HOLINESS.

The powerful dream of the Glory cloud convinced me that the coming Glory will contain the fear of the Lord—the awesome, reverent fear that the Bible says is the beginning of wisdom. This reverent fear does not manifest through outward good behavior, but through inward working of holiness and purity. We are seeing it already starting in many places and in many people's lives.

TOUGH TIMES, HARD PLACES

There are times in our lives when God calls us to step into difficult situations, do things, and go places where we are not comfortable, but an inner sense tells us we would be displeasing to the Lord if we refused.

That's what happened to Queen Esther. She had to make a very difficult decision. Could she lay down her life and say, "If I die, I die, but I must obey what the Lord is telling me to do?" Her uncle Mordecai said to her:

> *And who knows whether you have not come to the kingdom for such a time as this?* (Esther 4:14)

Through her obedience, combined with God-given strategy and courage, Esther saved the Jewish people. Who would have thought a little orphaned Jewish girl in a foreign country could win a beauty pageant and as a result save her nation?

> WE ARE KINGS AND QUEENS WHO HOLD A FULL INHERITANCE WITH THE KING OF THE KINGS.

ROYALTY

Like the monarch butterfly, and like Esther, we are part of a monarchy. We are kings and queens who hold a full inheritance with the King of the kings. I don't know about you, but for me sometimes life makes it tough to believe that we have the same inheritance as King Jesus. Yet God is calling us today to step up and step into all that He wants to impart and pour into us during this season of transition into God's Millennial Kingdom.

He is calling us into a depth of intimacy such as we have never experienced so that we become a formidable force to usher in the Kingdom with love, miracles, signs, and wonders. When we are operating in deep intimacy with Jesus, we are able to hold on to our full inheritance and the hope we have in Him.

> WHEN WE ARE OPERATING IN DEEP INTIMACY WITH JESUS, WE ARE ABLE TO HOLD ON TO OUR FULL INHERITANCE AND THE HOPE WE HAVE IN HIM.

A GIFT FOR YOU

If there is anything I can impart to you through this book, it would be to release an increased desire and hunger for greater intimacy, consuming love, and transforming encounters with your Bridegroom, Jesus. Struggling to be the person you want to be can be agonizing. Paul says:

> *Truly, deep within my true identity, I love to do what pleases God. But I discern another power operating in my humanity, waging a war against the moral principles of my conscience and bringing me into captivity as a prisoner to the "law" of sin* (Romans 7:22-23 TPT).

We desire to *be*, but are hindered in *becoming*. Let Him transform you!

Chapter 7

MOVING
FORWARD

At this point you may have some questions:

- ❧ Where do I go from here?
- ❧ How do I get prepared?
- ❧ How do I help prepare others?
- ❧ How do I know if I have enough oil?

All of history and all prophecies for the future revolve around this key thing: our Father in Heaven so desperately wanted to be close to His children that He sent His Son to die for our sins and unrighteousness. Jesus came to make a way for us to come to our Father in purity and righteousness. No other way could we approach our absolutely just and pure Father who wants to be close to us.

Jesus wants to be close to us as well, and the Holy Spirit is with us to guide us and lead us into intimacy with Him. Jesus is for us, not against us, and more than we do, He wants us to walk in close relationship with Him and fulfill the destiny God has planned for us.

> JESUS IS FOR US, NOT AGAINST US, AND MORE THAN WE DO, HE WANTS US TO WALK IN CLOSE RELATIONSHIP WITH HIM AND FULFILL THE DESTINY GOD HAS PLANNED FOR US.

We yearn for the wickedness in the world to end. Even creation is groaning for the torment of sin to stop, and the only way that can happen is for the King of kings, our Lord Jesus, to come, claim His Bride, and establish His Kingdom here on earth. We might wonder, "Is that even possible?" It seems out of this world to even imagine or think, but it is possible because He *is* coming for His Bride, and He is coming *soon!*

We are living in the day when all history is converging toward the moment of the Bridegroom King, our Lord Jesus Christ's return to gather His Bride and to establish His Kingdom. The Holy Spirit is giving dreams, visions, and revelations, prompting us to be ready, because *"the Son of Man is coming at an hour you do not expect"* (Luke 12:40). There is an increasing sense of urgency that we must be ready at *all* times, because we do not know *the* time:

> *For against its will the universe itself has had to endure the empty futility resulting from the consequences of human sin. But now, with eager expectation, all creation longs for freedom from its slavery to decay and to experience with us the wonderful freedom coming to God's children. To this day we are aware of the universal agony and groaning of creation, as if it were in the contractions of labor for childbirth. And it's not just creation. We*

who have already experienced the first-fruits of the Spirit also inwardly groan as we passionately long to experience our full status as God's sons and daughters—including our physical bodies being transformed. For this is the hope of our salvation. But hope means that we must trust and wait for what is still unseen. For why would we need to hope for something we already have? So because our hope is set on what is yet to be seen, we patiently keep on waiting for its fulfillment (Romans 8:20-25 TPT).

HOW TO PREPARE

Repent

Come before the throne of grace, call upon the Lord Jesus, and ask His forgiveness for any sin, resentment, bitterness, or unforgiveness you have been holding on to.

Release Forgiveness

Forgive everyone in your life against whom you may be holding resentment, including yourself and God.

Get Connected

We are the family of God and no one is an island. We *must* walk alongside each other, be accountable to others, and grow with them.

Reach Out

If you need someone to walk alongside you during your healing process, seek out those who can minister healing, such as counseling ministries, to work through areas of your life that are a struggle.

Seek Intimacy

Most of all, *"seek first the kingdom of God and his righteousness"* (Matt. 6:33). Fall in love with Jesus and love Him with all your heart, soul, and mind. Set Him as your first priority of the day before you are sucked up into the vortex of a busy life. Soak in His presence, and let Him fill you. Buy the oil of intimacy, and remember:

> *There is no power above us or beneath us—no power that could ever be found in the universe that can distance us from God's passionate love, which is lavished upon us through our Lord Jesus, the Anointed One!* (Romans 8:39 TPT)

We serve a loving God who loves us more than we can possibly comprehend. We choose how we respond to that inordinate love.

WE SERVE A LOVING GOD WHO LOVES US MORE THAN WE CAN POSSIBLY COMPREHEND.

The current season and time is one of the greatest in history. During this time:

> *Darkness shall cover the earth, and thick darkness the peoples; but the Lord will arise upon you, and his glory will be seen upon you* (Isaiah 60:2).

Through all the darkness, fear, and uncertainty, God's light, love, and Glory will manifest through you as you walk out your royal calling on earth to do the works Jesus did out of deep intimacy with Him. He is eagerly waiting to come for a Bride like that, and the Father will only present His Son with a Bride who is passionately in love with Him.

OUR FIRST PRIORITY

Be ready!

Be full of oil—passion for our coming Bridegroom King!

Know Jesus, heart to heart.

Be like the wise virgins, their lamps filled with oil to spare.

Be ready and waiting for our Bridegroom.

He is coming!

Appendix

Introduction to Soaking

Be still, and know that I am God (Psalm 46:10).

We may love to worship and pray, but do we listen? Relationship with someone we love involves listening, and the purpose of soaking is to help us learn to hear what God is saying. Soaking teaches us to:

- 🌿 Rest before Him
- 🌿 Listen for what He says (impressions of the heart)

- ❧ See what He shows you (impressions of the mind)
- ❧ Experience the reality of God

Notice we are speaking in the present tense, not in the past tense of long ago and far away. Communicating with God on a two-way basis is not just for biblical times. It is for today. Soaking brings the reality of God into the present in a powerful, intimate, and life-changing way.

> SOAKING BRINGS THE
> REALITY OF GOD INTO THE
> PRESENT IN A POWERFUL,
> INTIMATE, AND LIFE-
> CHANGING WAY.

When the Holy Spirit fell on us on January 20, 1994, I was thrilled at His presence and power. Before that time I had only had little tastes of Him at meetings, but those experiences put a deep hunger inside me for more of Him. Kathryn Kuhlman used to say, "The Holy Spirit is more real to me than any human being." I wanted to know Him like that too, but how?

Life as a pastor's wife can become very busy. I was so busy, I felt I had lost my "first love" for the Lord. Working *for* Him turned out to be quite different from spending time loving Him and letting Him love me. Yet if you had asked me if I'd lost my first love, I would have denied it.

> WORKING FOR HIM
> TURNED OUT TO BE QUITE
> DIFFERENT FROM SPENDING
> TIME LOVING HIM AND
> LETTING HIM LOVE ME.

When I married John, he owned a travel agency and was not in the ministry. We started a church in my hometown, and I used to cry and say, "How can I be a pastor's wife? I can't sing, or play the piano, or speak in public." In fact, I was so shy and intimidated that John had to give me three months' notice to prepare a message for Mother's Day. It took me three months to find something to speak on and I was so extremely nervous that I didn't sleep the night before.

Around that time I was given a prophetic word that I would be speaking to pastors and leaders and thousands of people. I must admit I was no different from Sarah in the Bible when she was told she would be pregnant at around 100 years of age. I laughed out loud and thought, *Some prophet you are!* (I have since apologized to him.)

My, how soaking has changed all that! Maybe you are asking:

- What do you mean by soaking?

- How do I soak?

- Why should I soak?

These are all good questions. Soaking is positioning yourself before God to:

- 🌿 Experience His love for you
- 🌿 Give your love to Him
- 🌿 Listen for His still small voice
- 🌿 Be immersed in the tangible presence of God
- 🌿 Approach Him with no prayer lists, agendas, or petitions

God is love, and He wants us to be lovers of Him and then of others. It allows the Lord to love you and you to love Him. Each time you soak, you experience Him in a different way. At times He will:

- 🌿 Flood you with His unconditional love and affection
- 🌿 Cover you with His healing

- ❧ Go back into your past and heal a deep wound

- ❧ Flood you with abundant joy

- ❧ Empower you for the ministry He has for you

When you realize that the Lord loves you, desires to woo you, and is enamored with you, your life changes, and loving Him just flows naturally.

LOVING HIM JUST FLOWS NATURALLY.

I grew up in a denominational church where no one told me you could physically feel the weight of His Glory or experience His electrifying power going through your body. Such manifestations of His presence are transforming.

While our goal is not to come to Him with a list of needs and prayer requests, it is good to ask Him to show Himself to you. At various times I've asked the Lord to reveal Himself to me in different ways.

Many times I have asked the Lord to show me things in a vision while I was soaking. Just recently, I was telling the Lord how I missed my dad and that I really needed one. A few days later, while I was soaking, I had a healing vision.

In the vision, I was dancing with Jesus. We were twirling very fast, and I was wondering where we were. Then out of the corner of my eye I caught a glimpse of a very shiny floor. Just as I was thinking we really need to be careful not to slip and fall, I realized we were dancing on the Sea of Glass in Heaven. The vision widened, and I saw a massive throne in the distance with smoke and fire coming from under it. A figure rose from the throne and began walking toward us. It was the Father! I recalled that a week prior I had been reading Daniel 7:9-14 where it speaks of the

Ancient of Days: *"His garment was white as snow and hair was like pure wool."*

I also knew Jesus had said, *"If you have seen Me, then you have seen the Father,"* so I pictured the Father just like Jesus on earth. When I saw the passage in Daniel, I was astonished to realize the Father looks like the glorified Jesus of Revelation 1:14.

As the figure came closer, I saw He had white hair. He approached us and said to Jesus, "Excuse me, but may I cut in? I would like to dance with My daughter."

I lost it at that point and cried and cried as I realized in the deepest part of my heart that I have a heavenly Dad who really loves me and knows and cares about the smallest need in my heart.

That is just one of many life-changing experiences I have had because I have taken time to position myself, allowing the Lord to come close and overwhelm me with His affection.

Soaking has also given me a holy boldness in ministry. The anointing of God has "made room" for me, and it will for you if you spend time with Him.

WE HAVE A HARD TIME
JUST RESTING. WE FEEL LIKE
WE MUST CONSTANTLY BE
"ON DUTY" BECAUSE WE
HAVE NOT KNOWN THE
VALUE OF STILLNESS.

What could be easier than to just to be still and know He is God (see Ps. 45:10)? Yet we have a hard time just resting. We feel like we must constantly be "on duty" because we have not known the value of stillness. Our goal has been performance and material success. From early childhood we have been taught to:

🌿 Accomplish!

- ❧ Finish the task!

- ❧ Do, do, do!

We cannot be like those who don't stay and rest in God's presence after they have received prayer. They miss experiencing His love personally.

We need to give God more than a five-minute romance. It comes down to the question, "How much do we value His presence?" According to Luke 10:38-42, Mary's choice to spend time with Jesus and listen to His words was an experience that could never be taken away from her. When you soak and spend time in with the Lord, don't be in a hurry. Instead:

- ❧ Put on worship music, one that helps you focus on intimacy.

- ❧ Get comfortable on the floor with a pillow under your head, or sit in your favorite chair.

❧ Turn off your phone.

❧ Grab a note pad for jotting down all the things "the distractor" likes to remind you that you should be doing and do them later.

> ## WE NEED TO GIVE GOD MORE THAN A FIVE-MINUTE ROMANCE.

Sarah Edwards, the wife of Jonathan Edwards, revivalist during the Great Awakening of 1790, summed up the effect of soaking so well:

> "I am overwhelmed by His nearness to me and my dearness to Him."

May this also be your experience.

ABOUT THE AUTHOR

 Carol Arnott and her husband, John, are the founding pastors of Catch the Fire. As international speakers, they have become known for their ministry of revival in the context of the Father's saving and restoring love. They have seen millions touched and changed as the Holy Spirit moves with signs and wonders.

Are you passionate about hearing God's voice, walking with Jesus, and experiencing the power of the Holy Spirit?

Destiny Image is a community of believers with a passion for equipping and encouraging you to live the prophetic, supernatural life you were created for!

We offer a fresh helping of practical articles, dynamic podcasts, and powerful videos from respected, Spirit-empowered, Christian leaders to fuel the holy fire within you.

Sign up now to get awesome content delivered to your inbox
destinyimage.com/sign-up

 Destiny Image